I0845883

Growth Acceleration

Turbocharge Your Evolution

Table of Contents

Growth is never by mere chance; it is the result
of forces working together.

Chapter 1. Introduction

Get ready to supercharge your personal or business evolution with the principles outlined in our Special Report – 'Growth Acceleration: Turbocharge Your Evolution'. This guide's easy-to-understand language unearths secrets of growth acceleration that are applicable for individuals and businesses alike. It's like your own magic lantern, except that here, robust strategies and practical tools play the part of genies. This life-enriching wealth of knowledge is designed with one purpose: to help you reach new heights of success, fulfilment, and overall growth. So why wait? Step into the shoes of those who have accelerated their evolution and start your own thrilling journey today with this luminous guide. Let's launch your growth on a trajectory you've only ever dreamed of!

Chapter 2. Understanding the Essence of Growth

Understanding the essence of growth demands a holistic examination that covers your personal life, professional journey, and businesses' progress. Let's take this journey together, delving deep into the dynamics of growth, its driving elements, and how it's intertwined with all facets of our lives.

2.1. The Concept of Growth

At the foundation of growth lies a multifaceted concept that transcends mere quantitative development. Growth is an unfolding story of evolution, of becoming more than what you currently are. This expansion is not focused on just one dimension – it is proliferative and inclusive, encapsulating all aspects of life.

The realm of personal development, for instance, aids in expanding one's potential and bettering oneself. This progression allows for improved skills, enhanced understanding, wider experiences, and increased effectiveness. It paves the path to accomplish more and to live life at a higher quality.

From a business perspective, growth entails scaling operations, improving output, fostering innovation, and maximizing profit. It showcases your company's capacity and potential to create value and increases market share. But importantly, it implies progress towards fulfilling the enterprise's vision.

2.2. Personal Growth Vs. Professional Growth

Distinguishing between 'Personal growth' and 'Professional growth' is crucial.

Personal growth involves expanding one's understanding, honing personal skills, acknowledging and addressing vulnerabilities, fostering emotional intelligence, and more. It implies ethical, emotional, and intellectual development. It's a never-ending journey into self-discovery and enhancement that reinforces your strengths, softens your weaknesses, and helps you in leading a fulfilled life.

Professional growth, on the other hand, caters to the development of skills, knowledge, and competency levels directly linked to your professional life. It comprises career progression, mastering expertise, boosting productivity, adapting to change, and thriving in your job or enterprise.

2.3. Growth as a Lifelong Process

Growth should not be considered as a destination, but a lifelong process. This compelling journey involves absorbing new learnings, fueling expansion, and drawing personal and professional betterment. It's a cycle, a continuous process of becoming the better version of oneself or an institution.

This cyclical nature assumes a profound significance when we consider mistakes or failures. Instead of being under-exploited negativity, they should be conceived as valuable lessons. This approach is integral to growth as it facilitates learning, enables resilience, and strengthens our preparedness for similar future situations.

2.4. Growth and Change: An Inseparable Pair

Change – often forming the crux of many anxieties – is, in reality, the catalyst that sparks growth. Life remains in a constant state of flux, thus demanding our own evolution. Embracing change implies evolving with time, adjusting our approaches to life and work, building resilience, and shaping ourselves or our businesses for a better tomorrow.

2.5. Conclusion: The Ubiquity of Growth

The quintessence of growth emerges from its all-encompassing nature. The transformative power of growth, in its ability to create a positive ripple effect, occupies a central role in our lives. By truly understanding growth's essence, we develop the perspective to appreciate this dynamic process, embracing the continual unfolding of our potential.

The journey of unearthing the essence of growth starts with self-awareness, includes triumphs as well as failures, and culminates in an overall optimized version of one's self or organization. Therefore, it's worth dedicating time and energy to fully understand this concept as it has significant implications on personal, professional, and commercial aspects. Appreciating growth in its real essence catalyzes a harmonious evolution, setting you or your business well on the path towards continual success.

Chapter 3. Breaking Barriers: Overcoming Resistance to Change

Our first cognition is the fundamental awareness that change is ubiquitous in every facet of our existence. It permeates everything we do and is a hallmark of our personal life, our careers, and the world we inhabit, both concrete and virtual. However, accepting and embracing change, despite its inherent inevitability, is far from simplistic. Understanding, confronting, and eventually overcoming resistance to change becomes necessary for growth acceleration, whether on a personal scale or within a business context. This chapter serves as a multi-faceted guide, providing insight into the psychology of resistance, valuable strategies for breaking the barriers, and practical advice for long-lasting, change-friendly habits.

3.1. Understanding Resistance to Change

The initial step towards overcoming obstacles is to understand their origin. The resistance to change stems from a multitude of sources, whether it be our natural inclination towards comfort and routine stability or fear ignited by uncertain outcomes. At times, inadequate communication of the essence behind the change fuels this resistance, cultivating an environment of misunderstanding and distrust. Despite the varied sources, this resistance typically manifests in similar patterns: disapproval, apathy, or even disruptive behaviors. By delving into these complexities, we come closer to identifying and addressing our own resistances.

3.2. Tackling Internal Resistance

Internal resistance, often characterized by denial or anxiety, can be the most challenging to address since it requires self-confrontation. Tools like introspection and mindfulness serve as potent catalysts towards recognizing and managing internal resistance. Proactive engagement in personal growth forums and conversations could fuel the enthusiasm needed to embrace change. Novelties and innovative pursuits, which provoke intellectual stimulation, can also work as counterforces for inertia, propelling forward momentum.

3.3. Addressing External Resistance

Whereas internal resistance originates within an individual, external resistance is motivated by societal and organizational dynamics. Overcoming external resistance often necessitates effective communication to elucidate the reasons and potential benefits of change. A strong support network, both within and outside the organization, can buffer the stressors associated with change.

This nuanced approach, bridging both individual and collective actions, encourages a shared ownership of the change process, promoting a holistic continuum of growth despite external resistance.

3.4. Building and Reinforcing a Growth Mindset

Dr. Carol Dweck's research highlights the power of having a 'Growth Mindset'—a viewpoint that views challenges and failures not as limiting barricades, but as opportunities for learning and improvement. By adopting such a mindset, individuals and organizations can become more resilient to change, perceiving it as an avenue for evolution rather than a threat to their stability.

3.5. Communication and Collaboration: Key Tools

Transparent and frequent communication becomes crucial in navigating through any change process. Being open about the objectives, plans, potential impacts, and even the uncertainties that accompany change can keep anxiety and confusion at bay. Moreover, ensuring opportunities for dialogue allows all parties to voice their concerns, ask questions, and be a part of the process, thus fostering a collaborative climate in the face of change.

3.6. Leveraging Technology to Facilitate Change

In the modern world, technology is an inevitable component of all kinds of change. It's pivotal for organizations and individuals to leverage technological tools enabling efficient communication, facilitating training, and monitoring progress to support the transition.

3.7. Case Study: An Example of Successful Change Management

To root our understanding in practicality, the subsequent sections will examine a real-world case study, showcasing successful strategies that have been utilized to overcome resistance towards change. Detailed analyses and key learning points from the case will provide readers clear, applicable insights to drive their personal or organizational growth.

3.8. The Path Forward: Preparing for Future Change

While immediate resistance can be addressed, it's essential to also consider future changes and our subsequent reactions. Developing resilience, establishing open communication norms, and promoting a collaborative environment are therefore long-term commitments. Adopting these change-friendly habits today fosters a nurturing environment for growth acceleration, ensuring sustainable progress for the days to come.

In essence, breaking down the barriers to change is not about the elimination of resistance; rather, it's about understanding, managing, and thoughtfully reacting to resistance when it surfaces. This continual process aids in creating an environment where change is not just tolerated but welcomed, allowing individuals and businesses to turbocharge their evolution.

Chapter 4. Identifying Your Growth Accelerators

In the pursuit of personal and professional growth, recognizing the factors that can significantly expedite this process is paramount. It is vital to pinpoint what we term as 'Growth Accelerators'. These are unique components within your environment, or nestled in your skillset or mindset, which when applied, trigger profound improvement.

4.1. The Anatomy of Growth Accelerators

Growth Accelerators come in various shapes and sizes and are not confined solely to specific actions or decisions. They can be mental traits or approaches, relationships, environments, or even particular investments that facilitate growth. Conceptualizing growth accelerators requires a holistic approach that encapsulates your entire life spectrum and the business ecosystem you operate within.

An inherently positive mindset, emotional resilience, strong networks of influential individuals, nurturing business culture, strategic investments, technological adoption — the embodiments of growth accelerators are as disparate as they are numerous. The task is to decipher these accelerators within your life and business trajectory, align them with your objectives, and engage them as catalysts to supercharge your growth.

4.2. The Personal and Professional Sphere

Growth accelerators behave similarly in personal development and business contexts. Although the specifics may differ, essentially, these accelerators comprise factors that induce improvement, create opportunities, or foster environments that are conducive to development. In either case, the accelerators might be innate or adopted, perceptible or deeply hidden, tangible or intangible. Decoding these accelerators is the fundamental step in equipment yourself or your business with a rock-solid growth strategy.

In the personal domain, growth accelerators could be traits such as discipline, resilience, or curiosity — pivotal capabilities that propel you towards seemingly unattainable objectives. Alternatively, it could be relationships with lifelong mentors, inspiring peers, or circles that challenge you constantly — connections that broaden your perspective and stimulate personal evolution.

In the business realm, growth accelerators could entail revolutionary product concepts, customer-centric strategies, or even the integral office culture — dynamics which create a ripple effect of constructive growth throughout the organization. Or it could be influential industry partnerships, market downturns that expose new niches, or the rise of novel technologies — external factors that could turn the business tide in your favor.

4.3. Unearthing Your Growth Accelerators

To locate your growth accelerators, profound introspection or an in-depth business analysis must take precedence. To help introduce structure to this quest, a three-pronged approach could offer valuable assistance:

1. Self-Assessment/ Business Evaluation - Identify your core strengths, quirks, habits, personal networks, or your business's unique selling proposition (USP), partnerships, culture, etc. Assess how these components currently contribute to your

personal or organizational growth.

2. Identify Patterns - SWOT analysis, past performance studies, or specific analysis techniques can give an overview of past trends. Identification of recurring patterns could uncover hidden accelerators.

3. Future Projection - Based on your current trajectory and future goals, speculate on potential accelerators that could be integrated into your personal life or your business model strategically.

4.4. Harnessing Your Growth Accelerators

Post identification; it's time to leverage these growth accelerators for amplified growth. This process involves aligning these accelerators with your goals, integrating them into your strategic planning, and creating environments that are conducive to continuous engagement with these elements. Regular revision of your accelerators is equally vital, as the dynamism of life and the business world may render some accelerators obsolete or give rise to new ones.

For tangible growth, it's not sufficient to simply identify the accelerators. Their potential must be fully harnessed, and the benefits reciprocated into every facet of your life or business model. Increase engagement with positive influences, adopt habits that boost productivity, foster a positive work culture or embrace customer-driven strategies — each action is a step forward in becoming a growth prodigy.

Now that you have distilled the essence of growth accelerators, the way ahead is clear: Identify your growth accelerators, integrate these powerful forces into your everyday routine or business strategy, and bask in the unprecedented acceleration of your evolution. You are now in the driving seat, steering towards personal fulfillment or business advancement at a pace you dictate. The power for accelerated growth rests within you, waiting to be unleashed. Unearth your growth accelerators and strap in for an exhilarating journey of profound growth and transformation.

Chapter 5. Creating a Mindset for Accelerated Growth

Whether you're on a personal journey or leading a team in an organization, the ability to accelerate growth is absolutely crucial. Driving growth is like piloting a ship across vast and uncertain oceans. The skill doesn't merely lie in increasing the speed but, more importantly, in knowing the direction and maneuvering the obstacles. In this chapter, we will be decoding the secret sauce - that dreamy blend of attitudes, beliefs, and characteristics - that constitutes a mindset for accelerated growth. We will examine how this mindset fuels the engine of relentless growth and empowers you to scale new heights of success.

5.1. Setting the Stage: Embracing the Growth Mindset

A pivotal step in inciting accelerated growth is embracing the growth mindset. The concept, coined by psychologist Carol Dweck, refers to the belief that abilities and intelligence can be developed over time. Adopting a growth mindset acts as a catalyst in improving your knowledge base, skill set, and overall aptitude. It extinguishes the fear of failure, fostering a space for exploration, learning, and, eventually, improvement. It opens up a world of possibilities - you begin to perceive challenges as opportunities, mistakes as learning experiences, and effort as a path to mastery.

Remember, a growth mindset is not a destination but a journey - a continuous process of unlearning, learning, and relearning. Over time, it instills in individuals a heady mix of curiosity, resilience, and passion for learning, sparking an upsurge of creativity and innovation - two non-negotiable ingredients for accelerated growth.

5.2. Becoming the Maestro: Cultivating Emotional Intelligence

The cornerstone of accelerated growth, irrespective of personal or professional arenas, is emotional intelligence (EI). On this thrilling expedition, EI serves as your compass, guiding you to respond rather than react to situations. It encompasses self-awareness, self-regulation, motivation, empathy, and social skills. When leaders are emotionally intelligent, they create a positive and nurturing work environment, thereby maximizing productivity and growth. They promote open communication, enforce accountability, and foster respect, leading to a vibrant workplace culture that stimulates growth.

Emotionally intelligent individuals are characterized by their tenacity. They see obstacles as temporary roadblocks, not dead-ends. This resilience buffers them from adversity, enabling them to bounce back stronger, quicker, and smarter. By considering setbacks as stepping stones to success, they hone their problem-solving skills, nurturing a hearty appetite for risks, and tremendous tolerance for ambiguity - exceptional traits that gear up the process of growth acceleration.

5.3. Harnessing the Power of Optimism

Optimism is the rocket fuel that propels the spaceship of growth. A positive mindset can dramatically shift your trajectory towards greater success. Optimistic individuals tend to view setbacks as temporary and specific, instead of viewing them as an omnipresent hamster wheel. Such a viewpoint encourages persistence and perseverance, building a fertile ground for growth.

Optimism nurtures belief in the future - a brighter future which you have the power to shape. With this sense of self-efficacy and empowering belief system, you are more likely to take calculated risks, pursue challenging goals, and persist in the face of adversity, thereby accelerating growth. Optimism should not be confused with overconfidence or misplaced positivity, it is realism tinted with hope, a faith in your abilities to shape your destiny.

5.4. The Art of Visualization

Visualization is a potent mental tool that uses the power of imagination to create a mental image of what you want to achieve. It conditions the brain to perceive that your desired goal is in your grasp, thereby galvanizing your efforts to attain it. This technique has been widely advocated by numerous successful individuals and organizations for harnessing the power of the subconscious mind.

When you continually visualize your success, your mind encapsulates this as your reality and propels you to take actions aligning with your vision. The nitty-gritty of visualization forces you to break down your bigger goals into smaller, manageable tasks, promoting planning and organization - crucial factors to spur growth.

5.5. Planting the Tree of Lifelong Learning

The idea of lifelong learning stands tall as a backbone that supports accelerated growth. Successful people are ardent proponents of continuous learning. They commit themselves to the process of continuously seeking, absorbing, and implementing new knowledge and skills.

Learning, in this context, isn't restricted to formal education or training. Instead, it permeates every aspect of life, including daily experiences, interactions, feedback, experiments, and, most importantly, failures. Nurturing this spirit of lifelong learning cultivates adaptability and openness - essential traits to navigate the turbulent waters of change, thereby accelerating growth.

In conclusion, the adventure of growth acceleration is less about speed and more about direction—less about how fast you can grow and more about how you foster the right mindset to facilitate it. The crafting of such a mindset takes dedication, focusing your unfettered attention on cultivating a growth mindset, enhancing emotional intelligence, fostering optimism, leveraging the power of visualization, and encouraging lifelong learning. Setting sail on this exciting voyage with the right mindset will not only turbocharge your personal or business evolution but also help you withstand the stormiest of seas and emerge as a more resilient and agile individual or organization.

Chapter 6. Leveraging Influences: Harnessing Relationships for Your Benefit

Every human interaction is an opportunity for growth; no matter how trivial it may seem, there's always something to learn. The prospect of cultivating relationships for personal and professional growth is a potent one. It's simply a matter of harnessing the power of influence that resides within each of these relationships.

6.1. The Power of Influence

Understanding the influence of relationships is the first crucial step in leveraging it for personal and business growth. Influence in relationships is bi-directional. It's about affecting change and allowing yourself to be changed. When you surround yourself with people who inspire, challenge, and support you, you have access to a wealth of perspectives that can enrich your decision-making and problem-solving processes.

Positive relationships can influence our mindset and provide motivation, fueling our pursuit of growth. From personal relationships that foster an atmosphere of emotional support, to professional networks that offer opportunities for collaboration and co-creation, harnessing the influence of relationships is key to navigating growth journeys.

6.2. Techniques to Leverage Influence

There are several techniques you can employ to leverage the influence residing in your relationships, ultimately leading to more fruitful interactions and conducive environments for growth.

1. **Active Listening**: This is an essential skill in any form of communication. Active listening ensures that you fully understand the perspectives and ideas of those around you, enabling you to gain insights and knowledge from them. It's about more than just hearing the words spoken; it's about comprehending their meaning, asking thoughtful questions, and engaging in substantive dialogue.

2. **Empathy and Understanding**: Empathy allows you to understand others' experiences, emotions, and perspectives. It fosters relationships that are based on mutual respect and understanding, making collaboration and co-creation easier.

3. **Constructive Feedback**: This is an invaluable tool for personal and professional growth. Receiving feedback helps you to identify strengths and weaknesses, while providing feedback helps to build stronger relationships, as it demonstrates your interest and investment in others' growth.

4. **Reciprocity**: This is a key principle in cultivating influential relationships. It's about creating a balance in the give-and-take of ideas, resources, and support, which can lead to an atmosphere of mutual growth and develop a sustainable relationship.

6.3. Building Powerful Networks

Beyond our immediate relationships, it's also beneficial to actively nurture and expand our networks. Networking isn't just about professional growth or finding new opportunities; it's also about creating a wider community where ideas can gestate, collaborations can be formed, and growth can be nurtured.

Networking is about creating connections, sharing ideas, and fostering an atmosphere where everyone is invested in everyone else's growth. Utilize social media, professional networking platforms, and industry events to meet like-minded individuals and potential collaborators.

6.4. Nurturing Relationships for Long-term Growth

The power of influence in relationships is not a one-time use tool; it must be cultivated and nurtured over time. Continuous and consistent efforts to enhance and strengthen relationships will lead to sustained growth. It's about creating an environment of mutual trust, respect, and support; a fertile ground where ideas can blossom and growth can thrive.

Cultivating influential relationships is a journey, one that requires patience, understanding, and dedication. With time, the seeds you sow today will turn into the roots of your personal and professional growth tomorrow.

In conclusion, harnessing the potential in relationships is not just beneficial, but crucial for growth. As the old saying goes, 'No man is an island'; we are all interconnected, reliant on each other to learn, grow, and evolve. By understanding and leveraging the influence of our relationships, we can propel our growth journey towards success, fulfillment, and beyond.

Chapter 7. Organizational Evolution: Growth Strategies for Businesses

Growth isn't an overnight process. It's a journey comprising deliberate actions, punctuated with both triumphs and setbacks. As part of that journey, businesses need to evolve and adapt to maintain relevancy, ensure longevity and cement their positions in the competitive market. Businesses are akin to living organisms- change and adaptation are the keys to survival.

7.1. The Pivotal Role of Strategic Planning

Strategic planning forms the underpinning of any organization's growth initiative. It involves clearly defining the organization's vision, mission, objectives, evaluation, and coordination mechanisms. A well-formulated strategy serves as a navigational compass, pointing the organization towards its growth goal consistently despite rough terrains and tumultuous weather.

With a clear strategic road map, businesses are less likely to veer off course. Instead, they will focus resources, consider risks, and build resilience in the face of challenges. The intricate process of strategic planning demands input from all operational levels within the organization, fostering a comprehensive outlook that allows businesses to factor in a myriad of perspectives, predict challenges, and plan for contingencies.

7.2. Embracing a Culture of Innovation

A culture of innovation fuels organizational evolution. Innovation is no longer optional; it has now become a survival prerequisite in today's fast-paced business world. It pushes the boundaries of what's possible, acting as a catalyst for growth by creating unique value propositions, improving processes, products, or services, and opening new market opportunities.

Creating an innovative environment isn't about arbitrarily introducing new technology or practices. It's about nurturing a mindset that encourages questions, experimentation, creativity, and challenging the status quo. Incorporating innovation into every aspect of organizational culture offers more than just new products or services. It fosters resilience, flexibility, and the capacity to keep evolving in face of persistent market flux.

7.3. Leveraging the Power of data

In the age of digitalization, leveraging data rightly is equivalent to striking gold. As vital intangible assets, data provides businesses with invaluable insights about market trends, consumer behavior, competitors, and operational efficiency. A well-crafted data strategy coupled with advanced analytical tools can unearth hidden patterns and insights, driving informed decision-making and creating a competitive edge.

While it's imperative to gather data, it's equally important that it is analyzed and used effectively. Effective data management and usage can exponentially enhance product development, marketing strategies, customer service, and even internal management processes. Optimal use of data helps to anticipate market shifts ahead of time, tailor products or services to consumer demands accurately, and streamline internal operations.

7.4. Fostering Collaboration and Team Spirit

An organization is more than just a group of individuals. It symbolizes collective strength, the sum being greater than its components. A strong, collaborative team functions like a well-oiled machine; it amplifies individual strengths, compensates for weaknesses, and drives the organization towards its objectives.

A culture of collaboration and communal spirit fosters innovation, improves employee morale, and increases efficiency. Creating this culture requires open communication channels, shared goals, mutual respect, and recognition of individual contributions. Team building activities and techniques that stimulate social interaction, build relationships, and develop trust can go a long way in fostering a strong team culture.

7.5. Implementation and Assessment: The Key to Success's Door

Once the strategies are set, they need to be meticulously implemented. The leadership team plays a critical role in guiding the organization through this phase. Tracking and assessing progress is equally necessary to gauge effectiveness, identify pain points, and recalibrate if required.

In conclusion, the strategic planning, innovation culture, optimal data usage, and fostering a collaborative work environment are fundamental to accelerating business growth. They can either form individual strategies or be combined optimally to cater to the organization's specific evolution needs. But remember, no growth strategy can bear fruit without consistent implementation, regular evaluation, and adjustment when necessary. As business landscapes evolve, so must the strategies. After all, true growth lies not in static achievement, but in the dynamic process of persisting, learning, and evolving.

Chapter 8. In the Fast Lane: Techniques to Maintain Sustained Growth

Fostering growth is an integral part of every prospering entity, but maintaining that growth and making sure it's sustained becomes the ultimate challenge. Down this speedway of evolution, keeping up with the pace while ensuring a smooth and steady drive is imperative. How do we achieve that? Let's delve into the strategies, principles and techniques that can transform sustainability from a challenge into a breeze on a highway for growth.

8.1. How to Keep Up the Pace

Imagine driving at lightning speed on a superhighway. You are thriving, accelerating, growing. But the fear of running out of fuel, the drag of friction or the threat of blowing a tire loom over your journey. The objective is not to just reach the goalpost as quickly as possible, but also to make sure you can keep the momentum going for the entirety of the journey and beyond.

In the maze of growth and evolution, facing hurdles is normal; however, to keep up the pace and maintain sustained growth, it's essential to always have a strategies under your belt. Strategies like learning from the industry bigwigs, setting and following growth markers, investing in failure and recovery techniques, embracing innovations and technological advancements, and nurturing a growth-mindset culture.

8.2. Learning from Industry Leaders

You're not alone in your path to sustained growth. There have been many before you and there will be many after. The ones who made it big must have done something right. So, why not learn from their experiences?

Emulating the growth strategy of successful companies and professionals provides a trusted roadmap. However, one size does not fit all. The secret is to understand, adapt, and experiment with the learnings that apply to your individual or business objectives.

These can range from Amazon's customer-centric growth approach to Google's innovation-driven strategy. These giants employed unique strategies that aligned with their company vision and goals, helping them maintain consistent growth.

8.3. Setting and Following Growth markers

Growth markers can be equated to signboards along your superhighway journey. They guide you, show progress, and indicate the right direction.

Establish clear, achievable, and measurable goals that work as a steering wheel directing your vehicle of growth. These markers should be quantifiable, like achieving a certain level of income or gaining a specific number of customers or followers.

Similarly, key performance indicators (KPIs) act as your speedometer. KPIs help measure the success of your overall growth strategy, or more specifically, your marketing, customer service, or sales initiatives. These allow you to monitor your progress, identify areas of improvement, and make necessary alterations in your journey.

8.4. Embracing Innovations and Technological Advancements

In a world that's evolving at the pace of light, clinging to outdated methods and technologies is like trying to race a horse carriage against a supercar.

Today, technology and innovation are two key catalysts for maintaining sustained growth. Whether it's upgrading to AI-powered tools in business, or adopting new skill-enhancing trends in your personal growth journey, staying up-to-date with these advancements is crucial.

Incorporating modern tools not only streamlines your operations but also helps gain a competitive advantage, making your growth curve ascend steadily.

8.5. Nurturing a Growth-Mindset Culture

A ship without a dedicated captain and crew is bound to get stuck in the middle of a voyage. Similarly, to maintain sustained growth, it's necessary to foster a growth mindset in your team.

This involves encouraging learning, appreciation of challenges, persistence in the face of setbacks, and understanding that effort is the path to mastery. A growth mindset nurtures resilience, leading to productivity and continued development.

Remember, it's not the destinations we reach that define our growth, but the journey we undertake, the changes we accept, and the acceleration we maintain. Using the right techniques and strategies, you can ensure a sustained and stable growth, letting you cruise confidently in the fast lane of your personal or corporate evolution.

This highway to growth is always open; all you need to do is put your foot on the gas!

Chapter 9. Embracing Failure: Learning Lessons From Missteps

Failure is as profound a part of life as the experience of success, if not more so. Indeed, the way we comprehend and process failure often dictates our pattern of achievements. Society commonly views failure as a symbol of incompetence or defeat, which fosters a fear of failure that can stifle innovation, hinder learning experiences, and spur reluctance to take risks. This chapter, despite all the perceived negativity around failure, aims to change that perception and to embrace failure as a profound learning opportunity on the journey towards growth, both for individuals and organizations.

9.1. The Myth and Reality of Failure

The popular notion of failure is deeply rooted in our psyches. From a young age, society conditions us to perceive failure as a calamity or a final endpoint. But the reality of failure couldn't be further from the myth. Failure, in its kneaded existence, serves as a learning tool—an unbiased mirror reflecting our missteps. It helps identify the gaps in our strategies, highlights our weaknesses, and forces us to acknowledge the need for improvement. It's not as much about wining or losing as it is about the process of continuous improvements and adaptations; failure is merely a critical component of that journey.

9.2. Embracing Failure: A Skill to Cultivate

Each failure takes us one step closer to success by showing us one more approach that doesn't work. As Thomas Alva Edison said, during the creation of the lightbulb, "I have not failed. I've just found 10,000 ways that won't work." The ability to embrace failure is a skill, much like resilience, and can be cultivated with practice and a change in perspective. By shifting your approach from fearing failure to seeing it as a lesson and a step towards success, you will grow as a person and improve in your pursuits.

9.3. Learning from Failure: An Essential Component of Growth

Just as important as embracing failure is learning from it. After all, there's no value in repeated, unlearned failure. Analysis of our failures can provide a wealth of knowledge. It allows you to understand what didn't work, why it didn't work, and what changes might ensure success in future attempts. It is a process of introspection and analysis; each failure is essentially a case study in personal and organizational growth.

9.4. Case Analysis: How Notable Figures and Enterprises Turned Failures into Successes

Many prominent figures and successful enterprises have turned their failures into stepping stones for success. Henry Ford, for example, filed for bankruptcy multiple times before founding the Ford Motor Company. He famously stated, "Failure is simply the opportunity to begin again, this time more intelligently." These stories of resilience underscore that failure isn't the end of the road but rather an opportunity for growth and improvement. By examining these cases, we can derive valuable lessons for our own growth journeys.

9.5. Fostering a Culture of Learning from Failures

For organizations, developing a culture that acknowledges failure as a part of growth can have impactful results. Those who encourage their employees to learn from their mistakes end up fostering creativity, innovation, and risk-taking. Such acceptance and analysis of failure can catalyze growth by inspiring employees to think outside the box without fear of retribution.

9.6. The Future: Preparing for Failures

The journey towards growth isn't a smooth ride. One must anticipate failures; they are unavoidable and come with the territory of progress. Reacting in a negative, fear-driven manner to failures can hinder growth, so it's crucial to equip oneself with the tools to handle future failures effectively. By doing so, we can turn potential pitfalls or setbacks into opportunities for personal and organizational enlargement.

In conclusion, failure, often viewed as the grim reaper of dreams, can actually serve as a solid foundation for success and growth. Embracing failure demands a shift in perspective, a willingness to adapt, and a commitment to learn from mistakes. Consequently, when nurtured with courage and resilience, the fearful monster of failure can actually metamorphose into a wise mentor, guiding us towards the destination of growth and success. By accepting this transformative viewpoint and employing the tools provided herein, you will be well on your way to utilizing failures as stepping stones on your accelerated growth journey.

Chapter 10. Case Studies: Real-Life Tales of Growth Acceleration

In this significant segment, we shall delve into a collection of actual examples, shedding light on the ways individuals and organizations have successfully harnessed principles of growth acceleration. These stories aim to provide you with insights and real-world applications of the concepts discussed previously, helping you to understand them from a broader arena.

10.1. Examples of Individual Growth Acceleration

Let us initiate our discussion by exploring the journeys of three individuals who have embraced growth acceleration principles to scale new heights in their personal lives. Their tales highlight the importance of acknowledging personal growth barriers, adopting a growth mindset, and leveraging personal relationships.

The first tale recounts the journey of Sarah, a struggling artist, weighed down by her fear of rejection and the societal perception of her profession. She realized that her fear was acting as a growth barrier and took the plunge to overcome it. Through holistic practices like meditation, yoga, and regular journaling, Sarah managed to break the shackles of stagnation, and her consequent increased productivity led to public recognition.

Next, we detail the story of Adam, an academic researcher. Adam was stagnant in his career until he stumbled upon the idea of adopting a growth mindset. Until then, he had a fixed mindset, believing his intelligence was a static trait. His new mindset helped him view challenges as opportunities for learning and made him open to constructive feedback. His journey elucidates the monumental benefits that come with having a mindset conducive to accelerated growth.

Our third exemplar, Emily, was an introverted software developer who often shied away from social interactions, which inhibited her professional growth. Emily's narrative illustrates the powers of leveraging existing relationships. Despite her introversion, she slowly started to network within and beyond her organization, participated in workshops and seminars, and consequently witnessed a sea change in her career trajectory.

10.2. Case Studies of Business Growth Acceleration

After a comprehensive understanding of individual growth acceleration, we now move on to business cases. We have curated three stories of different companies that have harnessed growth acceleration principles to survive, evolve, and flourish in their respective industries.

Our initial case study orbits around 'FoodLink', a startup operating in the competitive food delivery market. In the initial days, the company was grappling with constant changes in the market environment. Their savior turned out to be organizational evolution strategies, which comprised of the implementation of a robust change management plan and the promotion of a culture receptive to change. The startup not only survived the tumult but also emerged stronger, going on to establish its market dominance.

The second case study is of 'Zenith Technologies', an established tech firm grappling with plateauing growth. On recognizing the issue, the firm wasted no time in creating a detailed plan for sustained growth that mostly revolved around cutting edge innovation and consistent upgradation of skills within the workforce. These methods, combined with a meticulous execution plan, saw Zenith Technologies regain its momentum on the growth path.

Finally, we take a closer look at 'EverGreen', an environment-friendly business that learned the hard way that failure is often an important stepping stone to success. The company had launched an ambitious project which did not deliver the expected returns and brought EverGreen enormous debt and public critique. However, instead of succumbing to the setback, EverGreen used the lessons from this failure to transform its decision-making process, making it more data-driven and customer-centric, leading to a powerful comeback in the following years.

Hence, through a series of real-life tales, this chapter has endeavored to bring the power of growth acceleration principles to life. Whether you are seeking personal growth or business evolution, remember that these principles are interlinked and, when applied consciously, can accelerate your successful evolution. Indeed, countless more stories of growth acceleration remain untold, but these selected narratives provide a tangible portrayal of how you too can turbocharge your evolution.

Chapter 11. The Future of Growth: Preparing for the Unpredictable

Commencing the exploration in matters of the future, let's illuminate the context with an old adage which holds incredible wisdom for our purposes: only change is constant. This saying graces our conversation on more than one occasion, providing a solid cornerstone for our understanding of the future and its volatility. Trying to predict the future is tantamount to predicting the path of a leaf in a storm - a practically impossible endeavor. What we can do, however, is prepare. We can arm ourselves with the tools and strategies required to gracefully navigate impending change and navigate the tides of unpredictability.

11.1. Understanding the Future's Unpredictability

Unpredictability is intertwined with existence. Mother Nature operates in somewhat predictable patterns, but her vastness orchestrates anomalies - anomalies that evolve into trends. This principle applies to all areas of life, including personal growth, business evolution, and societal progress. Future is a manifold beast: a culmination of countless variables, foreseen and unforeseen. In light of this, the creation of an applicable framework for future prediction isn't feasible; nevertheless, a perspective and preparations for unpredictable growth avenues can be cultivated.

11.2. Agile Mindset: Embracing Change

Our first hurdle resides in our very own minds. A rigid mindset is resistant to unfamiliar circumstances and tends to respond to changes unfavorably. An agile mindset, on the other hand, is characterized by flexibility, adaptability, and a penchant for learning. It aids in navigating growth and fosters an environment conducive to prospering amidst uncertainty. Embracing an agile mindset helps cultivate curiosity towards future trends, a higher risk tolerance, and the momentum required to capitalize on emerging opportunities.

11.3. On Foresight and Future-Proof Skills

While the future's exact contours are impossible to predict, certain skills have consistently proven invaluable across time and circumstance. Leadership, communication, strategic thinking - these are all evergreen skills that equip one to prosper amidst uncertain landscapes. Coupling this with continuous learning helps future-proof your growth, providing a strong foundation regardless of the precise path the future takes.

11.4. Strategic Planning: Balancing Rigidity and Flexibility

While agility keeps us nimble and adaptive, structure ensures we maintain direction amidst the tumult. A balanced approach to strategic planning involves setting concrete long-term goals, but also allows for necessary adjustments in response to the unpredictable future. By breaking down long-term goals into shorter-term, more flexible objectives, we create a roadmap that balances rigidity for clarity of purpose, and flexibility for adapting to environmental shifts.

11.5. The Power of Antifragility

Birthed from Nassim Nicholas Taleb's intellect, the concept of antifragility champions the notion that certain things gain from shocks and unpredictability. Applying this perspective to personal and professional growth, true strength resides not in immunity to shocks, but in the ability to profit and grow from them. By developing antifragility, we are able to continuously evolve and strengthen ourselves - or our businesses - with every unforeseen hurdle we surmount.

11.6. Preparing for Black Swan Events

Black Swan events are essentially outliers - unpredictable and rare occurrences with profound consequences. Preparing for Black Swans involves building robust systems, developing contingency plans, and focusing on capacity building for resilience. Instead of ignoring or fearing these events, recognize their inevitability and incorporate them into your growth strategy.

A consistent thread runs through the fabric of this manuscript - the art and science of utilizing change as a catapult for unprecedented growth. As we conclude the final chapter, we hope to have provided a springboard for an evolving understanding of the future, its unpredictability, and the infinite possibilities it holds for propelling personal and organizational growth. With the tools and insights equipped from this manual, let's step forward to carve a future that's intricately charted yet fluid; a future that beckons you to embrace and harness the unpredictable, in your perpetual voyage of growth acceleration.

www.ingramcontent.com/pod-product-compliance
Lightning Source LLC
Chambersburg PA
CBHW060858260726
48661CB00008B/3326